God
Themselves

God
Themselves

Jae Nichelle

Andrews McMeel
PUBLISHING®

God
Themselves

[poetry]

Trigger warning: themes of self-harm, death,
mental health, suicide, blood, sex, violence.

Love 79

Contents

"i found god in myself/ & i loved her/ i loved her fiercely"

– Ntozake Shange

Everything

First Litany
of home

father, take us
>   *bring us home*

where the Thibodeauxs sell
boudin links from a truck
>   *bring us home*

where the air sticks
hot on my neck
>   *bring us home*

where they shout
how many? into our vehicle
>   *bring us home*

where my mother repeats
how many to all bodies present
>   *bring us home*

where my cousins & I
confer & shout 4
>   *bring us home*

where my cousins stay
>   *bring us home*

where sundays are greasy
& wet with sweat

father, take them
>   *bring them home*

my cousins & friends
& the others
>   *bring them home*

only if it's like you say
>   *bring them home*

where the city is gold
& there is joy

bring them home

I beg, where my cousins
are full of joy

bring them home

where I can join & when
I do

bring them home

I do with memory, I serve them

bring them home

hot links on their chariots

bring them home

where they peel back foil,
drip grease down

their hands

they are home

we are licking fallen bits of rice
from our hands

they are home

even sticky,
my hands

they are home

melting into yours

Black Girl Catholic

I like dipping my hands in the metal bowls of water & making everything I touch holy. Holy forehead, holy chest, holy lips. I am too old to sleep through sermon, too young to listen. Holy pew. Holy basket for offering. My grandmother passes soft mints to busy our mouths. Not busy enough. Holy sweet. She doesn't listen to me, but she will to the man commanding standkneel. We accept his crunchy bread. Holy body. We eat God. We eat, yet I hunger for softer things. My auntie won't let me see the Bible on her phone. She knows I play games instead. I dip my hand again as we leave. Holy me. Flick some on my brother. Holy us.

Choir Director/ God Don't Talk

I sing in the shower/ & the choir with me depending
on the angle of the water/ might sing Jamila Woods
VRY BLK or Big Freedia *Azz Everywhere*/ the first
words I speak to god are/ someone else's/ which is
how I was taught/ to pray/ my sins clog the drain & I
stand in them/ emerge dripping for my audience &
apply oil/ they do mix, do not solve/ I sip coffee &
crack an egg in front the sun/ on the windowsill/ for
my audience/ this my communion/ coffee my blood/
habit/ black/ the sermon is *You Don't Know My
Name*/ & it's true, you couldn't possibly/ I sing
because god listens to women/ who sing/ I sing
because I don't know what to say

                              I don't know what to say

          so I'm listening more

                    god don't

               talk   to niggas no more

          approach heuristic

          omnipresence + inaction is voyeuristic

     cryptic message, can't hear it

                    watch me, watch me, watch me, watch me

god musta been watchin/ when I climbed into the
passenger seat of that car/ colorless & model-less/ the
doors locked/ & the seats went all the way back/ its
hands & teeth ripped/ my body/ & the music playing
sounded like/ grief or maybe Wale/ (not that there's
much difference)/   My clothes pooled at my feet/
with my voice too/
I held the door handle/ like a hand

                    my hands, they keep score

                              eve covered up cuz

            she didn't want to be looked at   no more

                                   I'm either un or too seen, I know

                         good things   come to women

            who rhyme   & sing   (I seen the movies)

I aim to please   my audience   of one

                    my voice reverse-sirens

            I'm belting belts on

                                        mm   the choir

                         they got the right pitch today

Elevator

I didn't push the close door button
fast enough so now

I'm in the elevator with
Gawd

on accident & Their afro
threatens to envelop

me & I hope
They don't ask

about the way I anger-smashed
that beetle on my way here

I avert my eyes
because if I look Gawd

in the face I might ask
why They haven't anger-smashed

me yet & I might ask
about the dead & I don't want

that type of clarity—
let me explain the beetle

it was inside & I am frustrated
with invasions of space

& now I have my lesson, which is
the space could have been smaller

or no space is ever mine alone
the doors are only just closing

& I realize Gawd been holding
open, They were waiting (for what?)

I hover my finger at the buttons,
press down

Three Churches Burn in Louisiana

when two or more Black people gathering in the name of
preservation agree, it's a law. I pass two or more Black
people on the street, we form a congregation

built on head nods & anonymity. my congregation not the
forgiving type. an attempt to burn two or more Black people
gathering in the name of preservation

warrants my congregation knocking on your door on a
Sunday morning just to tell you your bloodline ain't shit.
now it's a law. a church is where two or more Black

people gather. a church unseen cannot be burned, it's a law.
my congregation resurrects churches & blackens your eye faster
than you can look at us. look at us.

my congregation don't testify against other members of the
congregation. that's a law. an embrace between two or more
Black people is silent worship of our Black

& our bodies. two or more Black people agree to whoop the
ass of the next person who tries us. I'm tired. I need two or
more Black people to embrace me.

we save each other in this congregation. we don't wait for
external justice. we don't seek restoration. two or more
Black people gathering in the name

of preservation have died for just that. my congregation
disguises a laying of hands as a handshake. they're praying
for me. me & the still warm ground.

Jesus Saves

10 cents (& the planet) when he brings his own cup to
Starbucks. it's just his hands, scarred & leaking black from
the holes. by the time he goes to drink it's all on the floor.
tells the same story all the baristas are sick of—bullets not
nails. pavement not wood. laid out for all the world to see.
buried. resurrected by those who won't stop saying his
name. he hears his name, *Jesus, your everything bagel is
ready*. he laughs at everything. everything. as if something
could be everything.

What to Do When There's Nothing You Can Do

I.
if you still exist   is it nothing
if you still wet your toothbrush with water

or spit   if you still
have spit in your mouth

if you still tweet
which is praying since you still

say something & no one
listens

if you still smile say *fineandyou*
if you still write

do you still write if you can't write about
what matters well   do you still think

anything matters if you still
don't scream if you still can't stop your avocados

from browning   if you still
try

you say *empathy* you feel exhaust you still
a definition of that one word

something you are   if nothing ever changes
yet you still & still

II.
okay, here's the truth. you were barred
from visiting her   so you described the world
to each other with words   you would say
the ground is freezing without you to walk it
she would say   *the gowns are thin, I am*
freezing without you   sentimental but true
you'd tell her what she missed on Twitter—
men are trash & people are sharing cake
shaped like kni—   *you can say knives to me*
knives & other things, you explained
she said   *I would kill for one*   a knife?
a cake! she laughed   you're sorry a plain one?
with cream cheese frosting   you want to bake
the world perfect for her
you tell her so *but you can't,* she said
though I'd love to cut it to pieces

III.
still, you find a mold to bake something globe-
shaped   it's symbolic
it crumbles on the counter, doesn't make it
to the décor part   still you try
to eat it   it cuts the roof of your mouth

we[1] create[2] our[3] own[4] coming[5] of[6] age[7]

---

1   first of the names we gave ourselves

2   dark-tinted visions, angle

3   limbs against the wind from car windows. we

4   nothing. want only each other. we're

5   first of the bodies we found ourselves. full

6   bellied laughter in parking lots & bars. when

7   is meaningless, there are always firsts to discover.

Beauty Mark

Beauty synonymous with Black
Black synonymous with *& then there was . . . evening . . . that first day*
Day I first touched
               collapsed into the folds of myself (to)
Self-love
Love is pieces & we are constantly searching for more
More synonymous with all that is God
God's touch, this mark.

From Her Bed

I don't know if my dreams are dreams or memories.
In both, I have no control over what my body does.

If I remember correctly it was a Tuesday & there
was something in my mouth that I now pretend

could've been M&Ms & I held them there
for preservation.

Last week I remembered I bit the M&Ms. *Sometimes
we remember stuff wrong* is what my friend says

but if so why is there blood on my tongue & why
are the bones grinding against it?

those are your teeth, she says   fuck you.

                    If sometimes we remember stuff wrong
                    then I don't know how to proceed. I thought

                    I shoved myself into my eyes & watched. No, I
                    wasn't there. *You can believe whatever you can feel*.
                                                             so

                    I anti-feel the world & just like that I am imagined.
                    I don't ask for advice. I keep trying to spit up—

your words, explains the girl I'm lying next to.
She holds my throat to coax them out. I let her bed

moan for me. That may not be true. I may have
moaned with the bed. She may have been forcing
the

candy down. I keep nothing in my mouth.

This may be true: her fingers
                           I reverse the anti-feel
                           a lack of blood
                           a flood
                           I was, once (I did exist)
          I admit

Sometimes   we   remember   stuff   wrong
sometimesweremememberthewrongstuff

haiku with alternate endings

something I want most
an alternate world that has
(no urgency, none)
(the sound of water)
(grass the only blades)
(clear air, rustling green)
(a black girl living)
(a black girl growing)
(a black girl at peace)

Lover, We Get Old

like we think we won't

& make scrap paper
of our letters of intent to die

I fold mine into myself, make
an origami hat

you, a paper plane—
a fancy one—with a Sharpie

you write *Lover Airlines* & it's cheesy
I laugh & I board

you're taking us to Argentina
because your time there

was good to you & I think
I would go anywhere with you

especially if we can ride
with my head in your lap & I can press

against your thighs & whisper
you feel good, alive

the aisle we walk down
reads *I don't want to be here*

anymore—in your handwriting—
so I'm glad

we're going somewhere else,
aren't you?

hands

by cutting—from the body of water to empty hands—
the audience knows I have given it up

without having seen me do it. my bad habits, multiple-sized
blades doing the work of drowning themselves.

applaud the trick. & while you look at my hands, you miss what's
under my tongue. I am not responsible

for the camera work or what you assume.

I still hear it, the lake. It continues as I do—despite
my best wishes. It reminds me

the opportunity still exists, will exist as long as the water
trickles down, to open my mouth, to lift my

tongue, to say
something honest. water, like a mother, can't

be fooled—always knowing, but won't say anything
until you do.

Sanctity: An Exposé

Historically,[1] divorce rates have increased.[2] Thesis: like gym membership, marriage be seeming like a good idea at the time. Then after a while you look at it & go—*ehhh*. They look at me expectantly & say *we are ending*.[3] I am wearing cargo pants & a tank top[4] sitting on the edge of my puffy comforter. I wonder what this means in terms of dinner. This time I have nothing to say,[5] though I have been through more devastating things.[6] My father's eyes are begging.[7] I refuse. Trying to look busy, I scan the app store for another virtual pet.[8]

---

1   as of yesterday

2   there's one more divorce in this family

3   marriage

4   a phase, unlike the girlfriend

5   who would

6   in my lifetime, after the end of Webkinz

7   *give me something*

8   to hold on to

Sanctity: A Consideration

I had on some boy shorts & a sports bra when I got married. Walked down the chips & cookies aisle to my love who held up a bbq chip bag said *you want these* I said yeah.

The lady with free samples of cheese dip catered & we danced, looking for bags of rice to throw at each other. Knocked over three packs of Chips Ahoy! cookies & she wouldn't let me eat

the evidence. Attached 6 cans of beans to our basket & joy-rode through the frozens with her inside. I covered her legs in Hot Pockets. *Dinner on me* she laughed shivered

I loved her. Our first fight was over bath products: lavender vs coconut. We settled on tropical breeze or something else we'd never really smell. She yelled *I WANT A CANDY*

so loud 3 clerks glared at us so I yelled ME TOO just to spite them & we got 2 left Twix. The self-checkout machine was our officiant
        BEEP   BEEP

We consummated in the parking lot.

the little g god of white things

is a barista at the coffee shop on MLK & 4th street
& is frequently disappointed by skim milk & the moon.

browns coffee with cream & serves
everyone with equal grace, cracks jokes only

to study the teeth of the laughers. as someone
points for more cream, the god blushes

& closes the blinds to the half-moon, who's jealous
of half & half—how blemishless & tangible its

whiteness. so easily held by tables, used
by hands. the god has no favorites, though

would say, if anything, if she just had to choose,
it'd be the coconut, cracked on the ground

like a skull, unveiling all its secret tender meat.

Question

I keep waking up & you're not.

I keep eating a plum & a protein bar. I keep making coffee even though I'm supposed to switch to tea. I keep getting in my car. I keep going to work. I keep working. I keep talking to people I don't care about. I keep being separated from the ones I do. I keep loving anyway. I keep my thoughts to myself, the ones I used to tell to you. I keep buying food even though I brought a sandwich with me. I keep drying my eyes, shaking hands, moving feet. I keep things I shouldn't—old receipts, a quiet anger. I keep my breath. I keep pushing air out & taking more in. I keep going home. I keep a bottle of Tito's by my bed. I keep drinking it. I keep pairing it with melatonin, with Nyquil, with clutching the sheets, with white fists, with heaving chest. I keep closing my eyes, falling asleep, dreaming you're with me.

repeat.

Tangible Heaven

everyone has something to eat,
everyone has somewhere to live,
everyone has somebody's arms,
everyone has their health,
everyone understands themselves,
everyone has this now.

everyone has this now:
time. with it, I watch the ocean eat
the land. I wonder if oceans are aware of themselves.
we claim many, but there's just one. alive
despite how we endanger its health.
I get in up to my arms.

everyone has somebody's arms,
so, you are in the ocean with me now.
(heaven doesn't require romance, but it helps)
in this place, we don't count pennies to eat,
you want to live,
we understand ourselves.

everyone understands themselves.
you fall backwards, using your arms
to float. *do you believe we can live
like this?* you say. I can't. now,
something eats
at me. I need help.

everyone has their health,
meaning no one is burdened by their self.
I don't watch what I eat.
when I turn to share, your arms

are gone. no. I can't wake up now.
here, you still exist.

everyone has somewhere to live.
you, in my head. you were not well,
now
I hold myself,
the water nothing like arms.
I retreat

to a healthier place for myself
where we live unharmed.
everyone has time now, but it won't repeat.

Prayers in Which I Type "Hello God"
& Let My Phone Predict the Rest

Hello God

        I love it
        & it was just
        like a plan
        for me & my family
        & my friends
        & you can do that
        for real
        for me
        & I don't know
        how I can get
        a good day

Hello God

        I'm not going
        as well today
        but I'm sure it was just
        like the one
        I had a lot to do it
        for the next one
        & the other day
        & tells us what
        we gonna make it out

Hello God

> I'm not sure if I can get a good day baby but I don't
> know what to do with it but I don't know what to do
> with it but I don't know what to do with it but I
> don't know what to do with it but I don't know
> what to do with it but I don't know what to do with
> it but I don't know what to do with it but I don't
> know what to do

"You cannot complete this assignment the day before."

& why not?
God took one day
to create the earth
& it was good

Revelation

I dream how The Dead return:
the marks of crucifixion apparent—

tired neck, punctured appendages, Black as ever.
Some, dripping water or red.

When They return, I fall to praise. I pray
to the ones who sacrificed their tongues

so I may speak one. I offer them my pen
& my hands. They be like *girl, get up*.

When They return, we walk for miles
without speech. Us, the still alive. Them,

remembered. When They return,
someone is playing multiple drums.

I hold my palms & my breath
when They touch me. When They touch

me, I lighten. They turn
water to time & heal Themselves, then us.

When They leave, we go with Them.

Everywhere

Second Litany
of girlhood

I. myself
I am called what I name myself   *I name
myself* free daughter, exempt from caring for
sons   *I name myself* the internal brightness
I was told I couldn't have, I have a story—I
once consumed a boy who tried to consume
me first & was disgusted; parents please
season your progeny   *I name myself* my own
dripping fruit   *I name myself* hot girl, captain
of the bad bitch brigade, softly   *I name myself*
without cursing myself   *I   name   myself*
something tasty, heavythick on your tongue,
something you can't pronounce unless I invite
you to refer to me.

II. a list of bad bitches I know[1]
Erin, accompanying me my whole life
Tolu, source of joy, inspiration
Hali, lifting me out of every misery
            I trust in you
Arianna, shaker of ass, shield from fire
Channa, fount of advice & wisdom
Mikayla, my twin flame
            I trust in you
Leah, expression of flawlessness
Hope, aptly named, goofiest ball
Hannah, master of the pole
            I trust in you
Shannon, keeper of realness

---

1   a remix of the Litany to the Divine Mercy

Lucia, sweet relief for anguished hearts
Ricky, clearer of bullshit
            I trust in you
Janae, who arrived just in time
Brittany, better than any heaven
Ariele, inexhaustible source of laughter
            I trust in you
            baddies, hear me
            I trust in you

III. & the people we should've fought
we name ourselves impolite. we bee-swarm
& sting our enemies. we fight [REDACTED]
as soon as he snaps Asia's pencil in the 4th
grade. we never die. we fight the teachers
who yawned as we bloodied our seats. we
swarm the schools in tank tops & shorts a full
two hands above the knees. we fight
[REDACTED] when he touches Asia's knee.
we never die when we sting our enemies. we
fight those who give us no other choice. we
fight them & we do it dirty, gnashing teeth &
sharpening nails to draw out red. we fight
those who call us out our names. o, my bitches,
how pretty all your names.

to come back

with a crown of dirt on your head

to come back from the stillness of your birth
back into your mother's womb to come back out

this time breathing

to come back & laugh & walk
& respond to your name

you never got to respond to your name
only told to you in epitaph

just in case you come back

Possession

I.

this the lesson: his hers theirs yours ours mine apostrophe S.

II.

the first thing a boy says to me is *you're mine now* & thus I am
possessed

watching my body wear her hair different
         & walk away from me
my voice is a whisper my lips suddenly only open when he wishes
    (I guess an idle body is a man's feast)
I climb the walls & people stare

my mother does not get a priest   she gets me birth control
& that's fine
I can't imagine my body   being possessed twice

my friends say I'm switchin up   my head tilts
                I'm no longer here

only men & god & the devil learn to possess & I to succumb
toddling to the altar to come thrashing banging pots & pans

this boy must think himself god   noticed me empty
& knew to leave me that way

how many tears & prayers must I release at once to make
water holy enough for exorcism

III.

his
my shame
a man's hands
my mother's stillness
their laughs
prayer's salt
god's quiet

IV.

if I say I am breathing life into this body   this dead thing
would it be blasphemy?
his hers theirs yours ours mine mine mine mine

Golden Shovel
after Lucille Clifton's "why some people be mad at me
sometimes"

when I die they will say I tempted the gun. they
will look at my body, bloodied, & ask
the gun why I deserved it. seductress me,
flesh hot & begging to
be pierced. the gun, I must remember
is just a gun. strong, but
easily convinced. when I resurrect, they
will say *witch*. say I must want
the attention of more guns. they'll come for me,
use my resilience to
justify excessive force. the guns, I must remember,
are scared of me. I am their
warm-bodied antithesis in their memories.
though in mine, I was simply born &
blamed for it. it's my fault. I
know they will eventually say I did it, keep
stressing how tired I was, how the on-
ly witnesses are remembering
wrong. the gun, they'll say, was always mine.

[some days I warm soup]

some days I warm soup   which means I put the soup in
the pot & turn on the stove to warm the soup which means I
opened the fridge & found the soup amongst debris which
means I didn't choose the beer instead which means I
cleaned a pot to warm the soup which means I found both
the rag & the soap or maybe the pot was clean so I decided
to warm soup which means I got out of bed & opened the
cabinet & saw the pot before the wine glass or maybe the
glass wasn't clean so I warm soup which means I opened my
eyes & didn't press undo which means I let myself feel my
hunger & thought of soup & warmth maybe I was cold &
maybe there was no wine just soup & a clean pot & my
mother's voice in my ear

What Happens In This House

is a child's name.

What Happens In This House asks to go outside/ is told to
stay in this house/ so

What Happens In This House leaves sticky trails on the
walls/ from playing in messes no one bothered to clean up

What Happens In This House stinks/ smells expired/ I have
to hold my nose when I walk by

What Happens In This House bangs on the doors/ presses
face against the windows/ is good at hide & seek

What Happens In This House hides behind misquoted
scripture/ & under bedsheets/ is home-schooled so that no
one else knows

What Happens In This House is growing out of control/
wraps around my ankles when I try to leave

What Happens In This House is a selfish playmate/ makes
up dangerous games/ dances on my bed when I sleep/

the others say *hush, let What Happens In This House play
out/* but one day soon What Happens In This House

will break it

[some days I burn the soup]

some days I burn the soup   which means I accidentally
unopen my eyes or I forget I was warming soup or I find
another task like my abandoned laundry basket & I sort the
clothes but that's all I can do or I was watching the soup but
had the urge to hold my hand on the stove just to be warm &
I sometimes have a real strong urge to be warm but not to
singe (again) so I hide in my bed where it's warm & the soup
burns but I don't

what you can choose about your body[1]

put it out of sight
put on it unbridled unlove

put it in a swarm of belittlers
put on it honey, shame

put it how your mother likes—jaw clenchless & feminine
put on it the lightening cream she bought you

put it how you like—come back to that

put on it a flower tattoo, but first think about it
            for at least 3 years

            (don't think about the scars you
put on it, unthinking)

put it in a joyride
put on it multiple piercings, holes

put it in hot running water
put on it Vaseline

put it on a party tray, invitation only
put on it bleu cheese or ranch

put it how you like—lips painted black
            arm hair a braidable length

put it in a blanket of any meal
put on it the cream or don't

put it in unbridled love
put on it thoughtful lovers

---

1   where you put it & what you put on it

[some days the soup makes it]

some days the soup makes it off the stove & into a bowl &
it's too warm & I'm not hungry by the time it cools down
    some days the soup is warm & doesn't make it into a
bowl & I eat it out of the pot   some days I eat some of the
soup & the rest rots in the sink   some days I even put
the rest in the fridge for later   some days I laugh at the
thought of saving anything for later   some days I'm
determined to make it to later   some days I'm not   people
ask me *do you eat?* as a joke   I say *no*   (as a joke)
    some days that joke is funny   some days it's not
    some days I warm soup   just to smell home or
perform it   people ask *why do you have so much soup?* I
say *because I'm sick*   they laugh   they think that was a
joke

From Her God

Lie down next to me
& we'll cry until we laugh,

make a waterbed
of plastic bags, kiss until

we asphyxiate, make it worth it.

I associate love with the kind of hurt
you smile after—

> Cracking your fingers.
> Deep massage.
> A little brother growing up.

Two truths & a lie—

> My first kiss was under
> a high-school stairwell
> I'm scared
> I want to pray with you

Lie still & you can feel
a subtle beating. It's the rain,

not a heart. See? I want
new memories. To hear *lie still*

& not think of stairs, school.
It could have been like this.

Lie still & silent,
near the window. When it rains

hard enough, it'll sound like
the universe is clapping for us.

Btwn Ur Thighs

I.
every flick of my tongue
is a rebellion
against you
I'm wondering if you feel
it as such.
our lips

II.
are the first thing
we speak from—   *mmm*
we say *mama* first
an easier sound to make
than finding our tongues
to force out *da   da*

III.
the first thing we remember
    hearing
is no.
been Blackmother no
(w/ glare= don't you try it)
been the first thing we want
to be able to say

IV.
the power is the N

been the sound of *n*   *n*
been the tongue pressed   *n*
    o   *oh*   *oh*
the eye contact.
we been dangerous—
the power of our tongues

V.
her name is Power
my tongue
been down
to bend
down to
be   in

VI.
been taken
I mean *no. n*   *n*   *o*
but I moan
but I stay silent—
been an easier sound
to make.

~~VII.~~
~~that girl tongue is a gun~~
~~that girl done shot you dead~~

I Am Angry, & I Will Not Go Back to Work

I have nothing beautiful
to say—I had a garden—

no, I am tired of things
not being called what they are

I had my homies—they were
jogging, they were in the back
of the ambulance, they were
trying to tell you something—
just wait—just you wait—

I have memorials sharpening
in my throat—they desire release—
if I talk to you, across a desk,
if you ask me about a 2PM meeting,
I will not hold them back—

my homies are dead—I'm trying to tell
them something, I don't want
to know the numbers

we've been wearing masks,
as protection, since birth—
my homies, remove them, it's time

we're not going back to work

I had a garden—this is no
metaphor—I had a garden,
it's empty now, the flowers
cut down to litter graves.

Gawd Goes to Jail

we all in police custody
thinking escape

> *Gawd's in jail*
> *for weedin'*
> *Their garden*

no moving suddenly

OPEN UP—reluctantly
last free breath take
we all in police custody

> *& for resisting*
> *arrest*
> *meaning*

> *refusing to stop*
> *taking*
> *deep Black breath*

trust me
where is away

> *when they tased Them*
> *They became*
> *sunlight*

> *& like moths*
> *they died trying*
> *to find Their source*

no moving suddenly

oxymoron: good company
memories erased
we all in police custody

> *so now*
> *They make flower crowns*
> *for caged women*

staring lustfully
> *like Them*
at melting face (*THE WALL!*)
> *knowing*
> *their bodies are graves*

no moving suddenly

see the puppetry
of this broken place
we all in police custody

> *but their light*
> *can't be dimmed*
> *by no dirt*

not moving, suddenly.

Gawd's Family Reunion

act five
Ain't no wedding because
there don't have to be one
for the movie to end happily.

act four
Gawd: *I blended some herbs*
in the kitchen. Rub them
on him & he'll feel
every ounce of pain he inflicted
on you.

(Dry-rubbed man writhes on floor.)

act three
Cicely Tyson:
Family reunions are about
glory.   *Us*   .
Women   *gyrating*

                                    woman

              our veins.
              What happened to us.
Black men   *Take*
Black women

                    &
tell them that you love 'em. Tell them.

act two
Mother apologizes for
perpetuating a cycle of hurt
& dependency with her daughters.
Mother ain't evil in a vacuum.
Mother & her daughters
go to therapy then get lunch.

act one
Gawd got enough foster children
to start a home-school.
Coconut-oiled & thriving.
The only conflict: who
gon get their hair braided first.
they call themselves little gs.
little g gawds.
Roll intro.

Prayers in Which I Type "Well, God"
& Let My Phone Predict the Rest

well, God

        is not a bad person
        but it will help us
        to go through this
        with the best of our knowledge
        & the best way
        to get a good day is to make
        my job bearable by cheating
        & making it something deeper

well, God
> I am fine with the following information
> for the first week or two of us in the house
> so it's all good now & I don't want to go
> where you are not going to be
>
> a good lesson for me in patience
> I have no doubt about that & it was salty
> for a long long long as I have been working
> with the following
>
> you have any idea what to say
> I am sorry about this but
> my business is a little girl in me
> that you know I am

well, God
> you can do it for me if you'd prefer to be in my life
> for the next few weeks or so I will switch to that one
> & then we can free ourselves from all the time we
> have to be in conversation with the lord of our final
> judges will not let us go to sleep how many children have
> to go so far in life that the kids are going
> through it all with you guys & I will be doing the
> rest for a while & will need to do some research for a
> while & I was wondering what you would like me to know
> about your name

Directions for Breaking Apart

a thin thin thread
called a screen
c o n n e c t s you with others,

a link

to   your   9AM
Zoom meeting

a
l   a   r   g   e   you are awake
bed

but   still   you
are   running
late

you've   changed   three
times   because   you   are
tired of the same old sh-
items
(censorship)

a thin filter for thoughts you wish
you didn't have

& now you
are not tired
of, you are
fired up, a
thin   filter
that works, a
change   of
plans,   you
are   not
running late,
you are not
running   at
all, a lack of
plans,   you
have
nowhere   to
be but where
you are,

a change

you move from the bed to the bathroom, a thin thin thread
called a mirror c o n n e c t s you with you, or at least a
reverse you from the waist up, how everyone sees you these
days, a face is being washed, a towel dries it, you do not
recognize these actions as yours, they are not, after all, they
are just actions, a consequence of existing—having to
consume, a meal, the same things you've had many times, a
thin thin thread called toast c o n n e c t s you with your body,
a crust, a warmth, you must remember to taste it or you'll
forget to, you'll just consume, so you hold butter on your
tongue, a moment, a memory of when you were hip-tall &
your parents spread things on bread cut in triangles for a you

no longer here, a reminder you can return, a reminder of the meeting, you are late but should still go, a consideration of rebellion, you are *tired of the same old shoulds,* you hate the part where you must grin & pretend about your weekend being *phenomenal & necessary,* of course it's necessary, it's a façade of rest, a thing you need & cannot do, a thin thin thread of responsibility disturbs you, there will be many fires if you do not join the call, except that's just a metaphor, in fact, nothing will burn, absolutely nothing, so you should have a second piece of toast, you should take your time & grab the peanut butter, you should brew a pot of the coffee you got from out of state, you should sip it, remember yourself

a   thin   thin
thread   called   a
window   p   u   l   l   s
you   into   the
world,

y y   o o   u u
must go   must go

so   you   go
outside

a   breath—the   first
one   you   take   all
morning,   consumes
you,

you walk into
a
transformati
on,   you
become
someone
who is doing
something,
you   are
running to &
away,   you
hear   a
branch   give
under   your
foot   &   it
sounds like a
snapping
thread,   a
small   small
sound
enveloped by
your
breathless
laugh.

Isolation of Self

love	l e	
efficacy	eff	
reliance	el	
pleasure	le s e	
appreciation	e	sssssss
assurance	ss e	eeeeeeeeeeeeeeeeee
awareness	e ess	lllllll
confidence	f e e	fffff
sufficiency	s ff e	
fulfillment	f lf ll e	
esteem	es ee	
respect	es e	
control	l	

s   s   s   s   s   s   s   s

e   e   e   e   e   e   e   e

l   l   l   l   l   l   l

f   f   f   f   f   f

     e   e   e

e   e   e   e

     e   e   e

I call on god when I
hit my toe on something really hard

god!! lift the first forkful of sugar-

coated yams *yes god/* check the news

even briefly *why god/* watch the sky

open & erupt *oh god/* feel my body

open & erupt *my god*

Now

remain calm   remain poised   remain strong

remain soft   remain lips curled up— softer *no*

remain approachable   remain pleasant

i say this with all seriousness: how do you not break the neck

of the next person who looks at you sideways? remain broken

remaining balance zero   remain broke   remain tired

i'd like a car to hit me, remains scattered   remain blessed

so blessed   *& all the time, god stays*   remain good

a dirty lying bastard   remain   *i mean it,*

how long must i   remain quiet   remain governed

all i gotta do is remain Black and   remain with your hands

where they can   *remain here*   remain   *remain Black*

remain   *here, unsettled* remain

Done in the Dark

some good things do happen—
soggy fries hitting a shot-full stomach,
2AM, I break from my 2-step,
shake some ass in the corner, lazily—
we stumble outside, she holds
my hand to keep upright
& I know. some people need the cover of dark
to be themselves.

I didn't like how that man
was touching you, she says.
then touch me better, I say
& she does. in the dark
of the ride home, while the driver asks
if we like hip hop music
& I answer, *sure,*

       & I do. only not when presented
       to me like an offering

her place, lit only by the flash
of our phones, looks like any other place
where people hide. she apologizes
for the dark of the porch
& we enter. she flicks the light switch
five times, stomps her feet, takes
my hand. *what are you doing?* I ask

& she answers,
giving the roaches time to scatter

———

some people need the cover of dark
to be themselves & that explains
why you only text when my dinner
is tupperwared, cold
& my bonnet's on. I know what you seek—

validation, not my body heat. still,
you'll settle for either & freeze
when the lights are on. how long
will you sit there, playing
at transparency? I see you
run back home. the dark

enveloping your back the way
you like. you shrink from sunrises,
so you'll never taste eggs the way
I make them. when you leave,
I close the blinds, return
the dark—

a threat only if you are afraid
of something finding you

as the bird

is made of glass, so
the stoner's smoke runs through.
thorough path of cloud—cloudy breath
rises the room. something so light, so light
obscures. so the water is cupped
in plastic, the worms are unsavory
parts of cows & pigs, plus sugar, sticking
to the teeth of the people putting the air
on seventy-one degrees. so the sky
is but a picture of the sky. as the bird
would break if it tried to fly

the little g god of alcoholic

beverages with only 8% ABV or less knows
about sweetness. says, with simple syrup slickness,

things like *maybe not those shoes with that shirt*
& tells you of coming out on the sun side

of a challenging childhood. she adds flavor
to all she touches & touches everything

including your face when she plucks
your chin hairs before doing your makeup

like the girl on YouTube (or close enough).
sweetness is sometimes leaving people

to their own devices, she'll tell you,
referring to her mother. she would rather

see you suffer than use Splenda. how she hates
phonies. she surprises you with tea

when you feel ill, & you thought you hated
tea until you taste hers. *it's all about temperature*

she assures you. *& just a little bit of honey.*

Singing & Driving

I.

when I glimpse my face in my car mirror, I am surprised. I forget I'm not the faceless machine I feel like. I forget I'm not yet spirit. for a moment, I forget I'm driving, that my lips move to a Floetry song. I'd forgotten how big they are (the lips). crooked glasses & acne scars. my mother asks me if not wearing makeup is my personal rebellion. truth is, I forget I'm not as invisible as I'm treated. the car veers, I set it back straight. if I crash, I'll crash still singing. once, an officer asked for my name. I forgot it, I go by so many. look at me. no earrings & a shiny forehead. almost forgot about my big front teeth. almost forgot who I was.

II.

when my father sees a car like mine wrecked on the side of the highway, he calls to see if it was me. I'm surprised it hasn't been yet—the way I roll with loud neo-soul coming through cracked windows distracted by thoughts & scenery, the urge to drive into a wall or tree enticing. before his phone call I was screaming explicit lyrics at the white Honda Accord I almost rear-ended. I tell him the wreck could never be mine. I try hard not to take anyone else with me.

III.

sometimes it's not neo-soul. it's a guttural release masked as an attempt to match pitch. a window I cracked with my fist. the Honda is a scapegoat for the people I can't yell my obscenities at. most times I'm only mad at myself, not the fact that you turned without signaling. sometimes the car veers & I wait to set it straight. if I go, well, I'll go still singing.

Testimony After Failed Suicide

& God said *anyway, you're alive* & God said *the way to give a sermon is to keep repeating & God said as if you know* & God said *as if you ever listen* & God said *why you got me talkin like this?* & God said *put some slang in it* & so I said God said *it's lit* & God said *I would say fire* so God said *it's fire* & God said *errythang I touch is fire* & God said *put ya hands up if ya know someone who ever been fired or someone who been fired into* & *look at you, how dare you try to do what I can do for you* & God said *it can't be fire you want.* & God said *this how to worship: carry memory of your dead without dying yourself* & God said *hands up til they burn—there's your fire—like you always on defense* & God said *cuz you are* & God didn't take responsibility for that & God said *you could've done it, ya know. must not really be tryin to.*

What You Must Do

To pray:

lie down—back against earth

only at night—see god is black

& blackness—share breath

with grass & thin mosquitoes—

with stars & exhaust—let rest

your shoulders—look god

in the face til you can't

To heal:

a black person never dies

once—they die daily, alive

then they die for their family—

then for Twitter—then

in passing time—I remember

running—into the street

searching the dark—finding

only questions—my voice

couldn't ask—stared god

down—lost

To laugh:

stick out your teeth—

show them hard & loud—

they may be the last of you

to decay—or the last of you

to survive—do you smile

enough—do you smile enough

coat your mouth in enough

sweet—make it rot—if they ask

your mother to identify

your body—will she recognize—

your smile?

prayer as edited by uncle ruckus

FORGIVE US OUR S[K]INS   as we forgive those
who skin us.

Forgive the inherent evil of this flesh of mine
this insolent tongue   that once crawled out between
my lips   to tell me   she was not made
to speak this pagan language.   I have been ~~fightin fightin~~
fight*ing*   her ever since.

I dreamt once of being baptized
& turning the river oilblack.
Jesus was persecuted & ~~Black~~   had the eyes

that Pecola & I prayed for.   Here is the house it is
brick & white it is   actually prison.
I am praying.   No, I am handcuffed.
(Either way, my hands   are where you can see them.)

FORG   E   US   OUR   SKIN
     GIVE   US   UR   SKIN
  OR   KIN
FOR   US
FORG   E   US

~~bodies without scars,   blood of hydra~~
~~so that when they kill a body   two more will grow~~

Help us to know,
Things don't Fall Apart,   they fall into place.

Sci-Fi with Black Lead

The movies are wrong. Time
is circular, meaning the future
is just us older in the past.
We are naked, we don't understand
science—we never did—
& I love you.
We've seen all of our terrors
before, so we rebuke excess.
This is enough—

>   gather sticks, set fires, be
>   together. Our families
>   have finally met.

We are still here. Your strides
slow and long, you bring everyone
apples to share. Where are the battles?
Behind us. Where we don't look.
Where are the men? We don't need
answers, but the ocean
is clear, gas-flame blue. So we ask.
Have we ever seen ourselves?
Look—

>   you, black woman,
>   still here, me, black
>   woman, still here.

How did we used to live? Always
on our toes & ready. One might think
the hunted would seek revenge.
We did. We rebuilt our homes & our feet.
Where are the heroes? We are still here,
only no one needs to be saved.

The Poem in Which We All Go Back to
Where We Came From

& it's a rapid unbirth. & we're back in our mothers
who are back in their mothers back in theirs & who,

depending on what we believe, climb trees or are Eve. &
regardless, we're naked & unlearn to hide & to shame

& unspeak our first words. & mine, I believe, was mama,
as would be my last before our tongues, if they

continued to exist, would drown in womb & water which
are both constants. if we ungrow, I feel,

the first to go would be speech & we would find
ourselves alone in the darkness of an unnamed place

we unknow & could never miss & could never explain why
it's not where we're from, it can't be, it is un

recognizable & we,   we're back,
but we're not us,   are we

someone's speaking a language we used to know.
they're not saying anything at all.

Love

Third Litany
in honor of the group chat

pray for me, y'all:♣
I'm waiting on good news:♣
♦:we're praying for you
♥:we're praying
♥:[sent an image]
♥:y'all, did y'all see?
♥:yes, prayers up for you!
it's down to me & one other:♣
♦:do you know the other applicant?
♠:did you wear the shirt?
I wore it, posted a picture on:♣
♠:I knew that would happen
♠:I said to gawd just the other day
WHAT, I didn't see the news yet :♣
&:♣
♦:also
♦:tell me why my mom sent
♦:& yes, yes, I saw & I can't
♥:I'm so pissed, I can't say
♥:& look at the governor's response I mean it's
the other applicant, yes, she's beloved :♣
always refills the kcups:♣
♦:it's insane
♠:your mom is funny
♠:will she send me some?
♥:oh I saw that picture, you must think you're
hot shit
omg how is gawd, it's been a minute:♣
tell your mom I say hello!:♣
♥:that kcup refilling bitch
♠:I second

                  & don't be mad that I'm fine:♣

♦:I'm having the talk with [REDACTED]
today, pray for me, y'all

♠:we're praying for you

♥:we're praying

                  yes, prayers up for you!:♣

♥:do you think they'll take it well

♦:& I saw gawd the other day

♦:still finding themself or something

♦:I think they'll take it well

♥:that's good, it's time

♠:if y'all could have any mundane thing never
run out, what would it be?

                        detergent! :♣

♠:& listen, gawd's going through some
stuff

♦:girl, patience

♥:why do you make everything philosophical?

♦:it's a good question

♦:detergent??

              of course they are, just asking:♣

                         I worry:♣

♠:mine would be time

♥:oh shut the hell up, who wouldn't pick money

                  detergent's expensive:♣

♥:that's why you pick money

♠:I just saw your picture, oh wowwwwww
you got the job for sure

                          time?:♣

            you think you're running out?:♣

♦:fair enough about detergent

♦:& why don't I see the picture

♠:yes, with my brother, still waiting on good
news

♠:pray for me, y'all

♥:oh yes, your brother, we're praying for you
                                       we're praying:♣

♠:the pics on her burner

♦:yes, prayers up for you!

♦:oh I see it

♦:okay that shirt is IT
                   hatewatch party next weekend?:♣
                       the movie comes out:♣

♠:yesss let's do it

♥:if I'm up & walking by then
               if not, we bringing the party to you:♣

♦:now that's an idea

♦:I've been meaning to come by

♠:I'll be there with food

♥:it better not be that homemade dip

♠:bitch, everyone loves my dip

♥:anywayyyy

♦:someone call gawd. ask them to come through

Corn

sucking the juice from a crawfish head, I like foods I have to
make a mess of to eat—peaches melting down my

wrist, eggs hugging stuck grits—that leave their memory
between my fingers, my sprite can a scrapbook of sauces.

much like my family members, I will not measure
seasonings & I made these potatoes too spicy. both our

eyes water, neither of us complain. so, now I know love is to
taste. if you measure it, you'll always short-

change yourself. if I did, it would not be the person who tells
me I have corn stuck in my teeth, but the one

who smiles yellow with me. I was eating when I confessed I
loved you, making a mess of my hands

& my face, unable to close my burning mouth. I meant I'm
not scared to be graceless around you, press my

sticky hands to yours, make purple with our red
& blue tongues, not clean up immediately. I remember

you paused to clear red-shelled bodies off your plate, my
throat thick with belated hesitation. you took a bite

of corn & smiled—mouth full of kernels.

prayer for you

may that song you missed the name of play again

may your money replenish as fast as it's spent

may the ink flow effortlessly from your pen

amen amen amen

may your enemies be separate from your friends

may mosquitoes know better than to pierce your skin

may you excel at anything you begin

amen amen amen

the little g god of aux cords

is never swayed by functional fixedness. she
dyes the ends of her faux-locs blue

using Sharpies, puts coffee grounds
in old pasta jars that now smell like arabica beans

& alfredo, hangs hammocks between two
utility poles. I'm saying she always finds a way.

she was once lost for twelve years before
someone found her homemaking inside

the cushions of a sofa & her story is predictably
tragic—cold father, demanding mother. she,

the littlest-legged sibling who could never keep up
& so stopped trying to. if your songs have ever

skipped, you probably pissed her off. it's on sight
whenever she catches the Bluetooth god in the street.

a connection without touch? she'll yell, fighting
dirty. *what's a connection without touch?*

as the river

drinks the house, so
it swells with whisks & whiskey & drowns
drawer-tucked secrets & the colors of a life.
lots of off-whites. some reds. so the sheets
& paint peel, so the ink unwrites on the paper
& it's fine. not all thoughts require
permanence. so the house takes a final
breath, bubbles like soap on the water's
crust & belches my mother's lampshade,
a TJ Maxx shoe, my thrifted coat. & we find out
what types of our things
can float.

I Imagine Joy

& it is a lot like jigging—
        footwork on top chains
                making sure they broke enough—
it's a lot like the painting
        in my grandmother's house
                of dancing to brass band
limbs loose & careless
        elbows left in corners
                backs arched to sky
cloudy from smoke
        of bbq pits & grills visible
                from resurrected smiles
I imagine joy
        as a dance floor that stretches
                to every corner of the world
teaching even the fish
        to milly rock
                so hard
the ocean turns over
        revealing the bodies it took
                never died
they just took a dance break
        washing us all clean
                of inhibition
& I'm hoping
        the band plays
                Casanova
                        so we can really get down

sometimes what I see

make me want to dig my fingernails into the earth/ & break
it apart til I fall in/ & reach a different place/ where niggas is
fireproof/ or at least proof that fire can birth instead of not/
& in the earth/ I find a god who is a nigga/ in hiding/ I say
we been looking for you/ they say/ *you found me/ now what*

sometimes what I see/ make me want to dig my fingernails
into my skin/ but I'm told/ that's not what niggas do/ & ain't
I a nigga?/ broken inside/ strong out/ how we bred & bought

once I dug my fingernails/ into my earth/ fell in/ reached a
place where I found some nigga/ some blood/ & in the blood was
some girl/ sobbing/ was myself/ I said *I been looking for you/* she
said *you found me/ now what*

This Is About Nakedness

I love you was the first truth I heard
　　　　　from my mother
the first lie I heard
　　　　　from you (but I am not thinking of you)

I am learning to undress with less hesitation now
　　　　　I am learning to say
　　　　　come to me　　　　　instead of
　　　　　leave me alone
　　　　　talk with me　　　　　instead of
　　　　　leave me alone

I am naked & comfortable
　　　　　you are bothered by my lack of translation
(that is okay) I want you uncomfortable
　　　　　I want you to look at your body
& wonder why it is still so clothed

I am learning to be open
　　　　　to say
　　　　　do not touch me　　　　　instead of
　　　　　giggling nervously
　　　　　do not touch me　　　　　instead of
　　　　　maybe another time

Do not touch me
　　　　　I am naked for myself
Now I know that my body is a language
　　　　　& until now I have not spoken
(but I promise you when I do
　　　　　you will not forget my voice)

I am naked for myself

I love you was the first truth I heard
     from my mother
the first lie I heard
     from you
& something I am learning to say
     to myself

Prayer in Which I Type "Today God"
& Let My Phone Predict the Rest
an erasure

Today God has changed since he was born & raised by his
father in the first place of his life. he had some sort of crazy
experience with his family members who were not able to
do it anymore & he said he'd have to go

Today God will be a great thing to put together for you &
rub your body in the middle of the night though I don't
need to be a little mad at Jae of the present & I was like
lmao okay so I can start another one with the same time lol but
it's fine if you don't frame it as disappearing but
moving forward to the next one is the best-case scenario here
in the world is our oyster & the bangas Thrifting
straws Marvel movies

Today God is a good time for me to go back to the Walmart
& get some more details. if you want me to send you a list please
let me know if you have any questions or concerns about the
TV she's been watching for a while I was
wondering if you could answer a few questions for me
about your opinions on the topic of African American
Vernacular English Department & how you can do it for
Ukraine & your family to go in & out of the house & my
family & my family & my family & my family & my
family & my family & my family & my family & my
family &

Today God is a good day for me to be a part where I am a good
friend & a great person & a good time for you & your kids to do
it lol you have to be a common person & don't
have a pic to do with US or other people who are in a bad state

& I was following up on my way to get the first time
& I am still not able but will try & get some crawfish for
you & I will get it next week it will take a couple days ago
to check in on my team of the team to see it & because of
that it was a wrap
Today God was in the midst & he had to go back & I had
no clue how he would be a good time for him & his
inability for him & to get him back in time for the first
thing to do with US in the next year & then we rent it for
the summer of our year of our final year & I was wondering
what you would like me to know about tomorrow & can get you
the details on how you can get a job & I can get you at the right
time to do with US in the next few weeks later in my

Today God gave me a good mango of the house & I was like lmao
okay

When the Last Time You Went to Church?

asked at any given family function. yesterday. a head nod on
the street corner. when I got 4 chicken strips instead of 3 &
I yelled PRAISE BE, lifted my hands to sing Ari Lennox in
the car. that's not what I say. I say define church—not the
group chat where my friends shout grievances & lay virtual
hands? not this chicken strip dipped in red beans? (if you
know, you know.) the last time I went to church I went twice,
the meal afterward like a second ceremony. what else is the
way I fix my mom a plate who fix her mom a plate who fix
her husband one? a food chain, us fishing in a pot that
never empties. everyone leaving full & with leftovers &
feeling seenheard. the question *when the last time you went to
church* not so much accusation as concern. almost like,
who's taking care of you? you hungry? want me to fix you something?

From Her Laugh

we cohabitate inside her mouth & don't sleep often.
cohabitation means various reactive warnings: glass &
tomato lodged in my foot. *I dropped a jar of spaghetti
earlier, be careful.* & various commands: *take the chicken
out the fridge. it's marinated—encrusted in tearsalt.*

with a nonblasphemous word for godly I could describe her
laugh. I would mop a floor for it. knock my teeth out & feel
it fill the spaces. cohabitation means we bleed at the same
time & smear it on the walls.

I like what you did with the place I imagine a visitor saying
& her laugh. we tell them it was inspired by the way cayenne
pepper tastes. the way we inhale it when we miss home.
funny thing about home—we never want to recreate our old
ones, yet we do.

we tack our achievements on the fridge: make noise, make
chicken, makeshift. make me still want to smile without
teeth. make my body a cake. vivid my dreams. god me. find
me another word, find me.

Complete the Sudoku

I	Do	Not	Need	You	To	Complete	Me	Love
You	Complete	Me		Not	Love	To	Need	Do
To	Love		Do	Complete	Me	You	Not	I
Not	Need	Do	Love	Me		I	Complete	To
Love	I	You	To	Need	Complete	Me	Do	Not
Me	To	Complete	Not	Do	I	Love	You	Need
Do	You	Love	Me	To	Not	Need	I	Complete
Need	Me	To	Complete	I	Do	Not	Love	You
Complete	Not	I	You	Love	Need	Do	To	Me

THIS WAS WRITTEN

AMERICA, somewhere—a song
skipped, so many feet lost
their rhythm, one could say
a stumble happened, there was
so many of us, was touched,
held up by someone else

there, we was, when this was written

there was no meeting of bodies
& pavement, only bodies
& so many hands, we was lifted up
into community-involved
love-involved
us-involved mourning
but wasn't that song sweet?
& will it be played again?

there, we was, when this was written

if a story is told
about us, us will be written
as if we didn't make anything
happen, tell them we did
we danced, we was, & distance—
a luxury neither granted nor desired

there, we are, still

How I Know Things Are Bad Again

not always,
your mouth leaves first.
I speak to you as if you are
a vessel for a later you.

I tell you about my day—
how a woman gave me
coffee free because
I didn't have change—

you pick at a plate
then leave it to dry.
lips desolate. I tell you
open, chew, push.

later, you do. food
straight from the fridge
where I saved it. later,
you might take a bath.

your eyes leave last.
you don't notice I did
my hair different. later,
you remember, you say

that was nice
of the coffeeshop woman.
I pour myself
into a glass for you.

later, you drink it.

Diary of a Sad Black Woman

I.
everything in my room is
             on the floor
some days you'll find me there too
making angels in the clutter
surrounded by Snickers wrappers & left socks
some days
I think I am an angel
most days
clutter
taking up space mainly because
I still want to be here
but can't seem to pick myself up

II.
at 7:59 I retweet a gif of Viola Davis taking off her wig after
crying. when I saw it I thought it a metaphor for how
completely stripped away I feel but I comment *lol same
@afriend.* at 8:12 I post a picture of a meal I'll never finish
then ask *anyone know of some good queer Black movies?* by
which I mean *are there any examples of a life like mine that
ends happily* & the answer is no. 10:15 I retweet an article
about the movement or something else #important. Black
girls live in a world where both living & dying are
revolutionary acts & neither is the obvious choice. Instead of
dying today I type *man I really need a day off* or I [gif of
animal doing something adorably human] or I diary via
subtweets. I make jokes that only I understand. I am talking
to everyone & no one [laughing emoji]. I use the laughing
emoji & the crying emoji interchangeably. at 11:40 I tweet
goodnight which people don't do anymore but I just need
someone to say it to.

Watches Paint Dry

loving me must feel like
  — this
  — waiting so long for something to change
  — a hesitant gauging touch
  — explaining gender to that one auntie

I'm trying to say I know it's hard

you picked me flowers
  — they are beautiful
  — but I've already seen too many beautiful things die

Worthy of Praise

I.
notice me now,
body shimmering.
much like the moon, I demand
admiration. you cannot handle
me in full, so you try
to break me into pieces.

II.
you thought I would ripple
like water when you touched
me, but I am much stronger
than I seem.
unwavering against
even the hardest of things.

III.
there. I was almost nothing.
limbs roots that snap quick.
I cannot carry you,
just your gaze.
what will be left of you
when I take back all I gave?

MAYBE: GOD

I.

the existence of bad words implies good ones. you believe saying *yes* is good even when you don't want to. if there are bad girls who curse & spit & sit like men then there are good girls who don't. you wonder if girls & words are ever just those things without dichotomy. you spend a lot of time closed—your legs & your lips—trying out goodness. god, like any parent, will be very nice to you until displeased, you learn. you say *yes*, you don't have much space to take up anyway. it is before the iPhone & you only have 200 texts a month to use sparingly. you make each one count so as not to spark a back & forth you'd have to pay for. never *I feel* only *yes okay sorry*. all arguments cost you something. plus, you learn, anyone bigger than you can tell you what to do. a boy bigger than you says *be a good girl, don't say a word.* you reassess—there are no good words. girls are good when silent & open at the command of someone bigger. god is good, see how god is silent? you should be smaller than everyone. parents, like any god, speak in parables. *bad girls end up dead or on the streets.* they do not mention who killed them, who closed their doors. your phone bill comes, rewards your lack of questions. your parents call. you are scared to pick up.

II.

a good listener is just a bad conversationalist. so my arguments with god are one-sided long paragraphs to which I see *read at [day/ time]*. I am proud to admit I speak enough to have my phone determine my frequently used words. so by now I can use predictive text to pray—

Hello

God

Dammit

I

Am

Still

Trying

To

Talk

About

It

With

My

Mother

OK

For Pecola
of Toni Morrison's *The Bluest Eye*

Here is the house. It is brick & white. It is very pretty. It is empty. Father is groaning. *Won't be back till late, won't be back.* Groan, Father, groan. Mother cries. *Don't be back.* Cry, mother, cry. See Little Brother, he is playing. Spades for money & 21 (his age backwards) on a makeshift table. Rat races—the new Mario Kart. Play, Brother, Play. Mother, Father, Brother, & Pecola pay for the brick & white house. Pecola is naked, why is Pecola naked?

here is the house it is brick & white you are very pretty you are empty. You are groaning. *Won't be back till late, won't be back.* You cry. *You were never here.* Cry, You, cry. You are selling more than a body to live in the brick & white house. Little Brother plays Operation on a girl or vice versa. Father is getting ready for work. He is playing dress up. You are hiding. No one is searching. Play Family, play.

herewasthehouseitwasbrickandwhiteitwasbrickandwhiteitw
asveryprettyitwasemptyitwasemptyitwasitwas

Barefoot Duplex

I am starting to forget how to walk
barefoot. we are holiest when our feet touch ground.

                barefoot, we are holy. our feet touch
                under the table & I say I love you aloud.

under the table, I am allowed to love you.
I dream up a life we could have.

                oh, how much living we could do
                if not for those who would kill us.

it kills me, those who are not for us.
heaven is so far, they say.

                I say, so far, heaven is
                us going nowhere else when we get home.

I think of going away from this home.
I start to forget how to walk.

(The Play)
    After the gospel musical *I Know I've Been Changed*

Act One
God got
this me
got me
down out
of luck
drugs got
me God
my God
my knock
life down
got God?
I mean
got drugs
song interlude
run with
my voice
with my
legs with
my God
got me
here my
self God
me here
see the
woman life
here? got
down got
mean run
song interlude

Act Two
I sing because
God listens to
women who sing
I sing because
I cannot yell
I run because
I tried cry
& it don't
work & work
don't neither so
praise break from
broken mouth cracked
lips sing too
abuse is result
of God-lack
let's find God
in these lines
I sing us
together *song interlude*

Act Three
heaven forbid a man
be a(p)parent or a
young mother be a
success the lesson is
be less free woman
be server less lip
woman know closed-mouths
don't get cracked open
& the lesson of
the power of a
woman's word this whole
world started with a
woman's word I say
that's how it all
will end *final song*

Psalm 161:
Praise for the People at the End of the World[1]

'akeem

1 'bout some months ago,
   we lost track of the months.
2 'twas Zeena who told me
   the people—
3 'scuse me, it's hard to say—
   the people will be gone.
4 'tis the real true end
   of everything. my god, it take
5 'em all to tell the story,
   the people I praise.
6 'ear, if you have ears,
   what happened. it's quiet.
7 'round here was—
   we kept our word, it's quiet
8 'cuz we all that's left,
   & the trees, I want to say—

veronica

9 voices! I miss the sound
   of fucking people. I'm on the
10 verge of—I don't know—
   I crunched the leaves to mimic steps.
11 vain as I was, I can't see
   why god kept me here but for
12 vengeance. I am alone
   & don't love myself in a

13 vacuum. I miss my love, we
   kept our word though. it's all
14 vacant now. you want to know?
   I'll tell you this—all this shit
15 vanished slowly, but not
   by fire or
16 vices or whatever they told you.
   it was us, remember that.

gabi

17 going back to the beginning,
   my mom & me
18 got the call from talon—
   we want to
19 *go out with a bang.*
   how he knew, I didn't ask.
20 god, I assume, forgives
   when you have a
21 good reason. we robbed
   the rich. it's funny,
22 guess what my mom bought first?
   a bidet.
23 giggled the whole way home,
   talking 'bout *when they*
24 *gaze at my body, cold, they should see*
   my ass in all its glory.

---

1   This poem takes its form from the biblical Psalm 119, which is an acrostic of the
    Hebrew alphabet.

de'man

25 damn, I thought they would
   kill us when we started
26 doling out the money. wait,
   I want my last words to be
27 different. I'm starting over.
   I'll tell you about
28 dewan, my brother.
   even in prison he
29 did what any brother would—
   helped me with homework. though I
30 didn't get the answers
   till weeks after in the mail. when he'd
31 done his time, he told me
   these words:
32 *death ain't shit but freedom, no need*
   to involve a god.

hunny

33 here, they'll ban guns
   soon as the person
34 holding one looks like us. hm,
   what would you do if you
35 had the money you needed?
   I ate. ate till
36 hunger forgot me. I'd been
   so long away from full it
37 hurt. we wanted to be
   satisfied, that's what people
38 hunt for, not blood. something
   that feels right.

39 *have mercy*, one of the women
   said to me. I'm no god.
40 have mercy. while she clutched
   her necklace & my stomach growled.

wesley

41 we kept our word.
   we
42 wondered what they would do—
   come for us? we
43 waited for god & them,
   no one came. maybe they
44 wanted us to steal from them,
   give them some
45 way to feel persecuted
   or pity. we
46 worked so hard
   for so little. this is not about
47 what they had, we
   were told *wait wait wait*
48 when? god,
   till when?

zeena

49 zealously we lived on
   until the money meant
50 zilch. there was something
   in the air & we watched—
51 zany theory by theory—people go.
   those of us left know soon

⁵² zero of us will remain.
    we are undead, not
⁵³ zombified but in the between part
    when life is still here but all
⁵⁴ zest for it leaves. we stopped
    digging, I don't move from this
⁵⁵ zone of bodilessness. maybe it means
    something to god that our
⁵⁶ zenith came to this—
    a spectacular nadir.

chance

⁵⁷ change don't happen overnight
    'til it does. we think we got
⁵⁸ choices, right? ma used to say to me
    you end up where you
⁵⁹ choose to be. who chose for me
    to exist? not me, never got the
⁶⁰ chance to choose to not work, to travel,
    to spend my
⁶¹ childhood a child.
    I can't control all that's
⁶² changed on me, just my response
    to it & now look. you think all
⁶³ change is by god? or do we
    say that cuz we don't have a
⁶⁴ choice?
    hm?

talon

⁶⁵ to everyone who asks I say
    maybe god
⁶⁶ told me. I was the first
    to know what was coming,
⁶⁷ tasked with spreading the word.
    gabi will
⁶⁸ tell you about the bang.
    I only wanted the
⁶⁹ tables turned. I lost
    so many I stopped
⁷⁰ tallying the bodies, stopped
    checking the cribs, tracking
⁷¹ time.
    please, if this was a test, god,
⁷² take me soon.
    I don't know what's true.

yessimi

⁷³ yes, for a moment
    the people deserved praise.
⁷⁴ you should have seen it,
    before the numbers dwindled
⁷⁵ young people made peace
    with god, themselves
⁷⁶ yelled into the night
    at their parties
⁷⁷ yanked each other into corners,
    forgave their parents. my
⁷⁸ youngest called—
    first time in seven

⁷⁹ years—to say *I love you*.
    I've made so many mistakes,
⁸⁰ yearned for understanding
    & grace came, came knocking.

karla

⁸¹ candlelight. after the end
    is a return to the beginning.
⁸² chronologically, it goes—
    in terms of loss—electricity,
⁸³ cars, decorum. we saw the end
    of law, a glimpse of
⁸⁴ care for others, everyone
    fed & without luxury,
⁸⁵ comforted, for a moment,
    by sameness. if birds are here, they're
⁸⁶ keeping quiet, watching us
    perish. we
⁸⁷ kept our word, lit candles,
    pulled our
⁸⁸ kin
    close.

lianne

⁸⁹ look, here's the truth.
    everyone acts so resigned. if you
⁹⁰ listen, you can hear
    the heartache. even those who
⁹¹ long for the world to end
    don't want it so. they want
⁹² liberation. they want people

    to touch them & their
⁹³ lives to mean something.
    no one gains peace from
⁹⁴ loveless silence. god?
    god is
⁹⁵ laughing at us. I am angry
    & unafraid to admit I've
⁹⁶ lost so much & no,
    it never gets easier to lose.

maya

⁹⁷ my sister
    has lost her
⁹⁸ mind. but before,
    she was lively,
⁹⁹ model-type with cat eyes
    that could slice you open.
¹⁰⁰ made every day an event. the parties?
    sickening. god, she
¹⁰¹ mentioned wanting to *be someone*
    repeatedly, I
¹⁰² mistakenly never told her
    she was. so
¹⁰³ many times I could've—
    I can't say. I hum her
¹⁰⁴ music I can remember,
    sing her songs she knows.

nakaya

[105] need you? no,
   I am a god. I'm
[106] not
   letting go. I
[107] never
   let a broke bitch—
[108] never
   would have made it! my
[109] nigga
   the
[110] night is
   still young, you
[111] nasty, you nasty, what my sister
   say? I miss the
[112] noise
   of everything.

sage

[113] some of us wanted more
   from our last days, I'll
[114] say that. there's so much
   I won't get to
[115] see now. I bought
   a boat, a small one, to
[116] sail to somewhere
   unfamiliar, not stress over
[117] spending money or time,
   let god's
[118] sun brown me further. but alone
   as I am I never did

[119] surrender a desire for roots
   so I'm here, I
[120] stayed, & anyway
   I know nothing about the sea.

knix

[121] psalm for the people:
   when I say we, I mean those who
[122] knew the true cost
   of living. we are, all of us,
[123] wretched for reasons
   we can't control, though our
[124] psyches say we must try to pilot
   our lives. I grieve even the least
[125] honest of us, who, though not absolved,
   were products of the expectations
[126] gnawing at their necks. by god, we rioted,
   we slept, we succumbed to
[127] wrought divisions, we
   were ambitious, foolishly tracking
[128] hours as if we
   could ever know the time.

prince

[129] people will mention the loss.
   I want to
[130] point out this moment—
   my son, hip-tall, missing teeth,
[131] planted a peony seed
   in our garden. I'd explained our
[132] predicament before, how soon
   we will drop, peacefully, like

[133] paw paw & maw maw
& that's alright. I
[134] prepared to remind him, he then said
it doesn't need me here to grow. so we
[135] populated our small land with the rest
of our life. when he went, I
[136] placed him with god
among the seeds.

tsamuel

[137] tsk,
I've no sob story, no bes-
[138] tseller to list out for you.
the world is no accident, just craf-
[139] tsmanship. so is this
& everything else. we'd be collectivis-
[140] ts if evolution equaled
survival, but no, we are too shor-
[141] tsighted for anything to last,
including ourselves. I say we ou-
[142] tsourced too many emotions—happiness,
love, belonging—our descendan-
[143] ts predestined for demise.
god, if listening, ou-
[144] tstretch
your hands.

quinton

[145] quiet now, but I hear
so many final re-
[146] quests—*I need to get right*

with god. bury me
[147] *quickly. wait.* I was & wasn't
ready for the
[148] queasiness in my throat.
were we correct? a
[149] question for god. though divine input
never comes
[150] quite like you'd think. it was
& wasn't how I imagined. still, I
[151] quell their voices
with baseless hope.
[152] quote me on this:
we kept our word.

re'shawn

[153] rally the people
hear their cries
[154] ragtag misfits
organize. they
[155] ran us down
with fear & lies
[156] right now we all
reclaim our lives
[157] rise, rise
raise our fists & voices high
[158] refrain from
taking compromise
[159] renounce our choices,
true reprise
[160] rebuild rebuild
till god replies

charlotte

161 shit yeah, I bought
    that bidet when we were
162 sure it would come to
    what it came to. always thought I
163 should go out in style—
    fur, face beat, silk
164 shirt for comfort, slightly unbuttoned
    to convince the
165 shepherd I was
    a good girl. no
166 shame in wanting to die
    fabulous when life
167 short-changed me.
    & why wouldn't I
168 show out to greet god? that's
    a once-in-a-lifetime event.

tiny

169 today it's quiet
    but for the trees, which
170 taunt their unaffiliation.
    life did not begin with
171 two people, but none,
    so without us will continue.
172 tomorrow, no one to remember
    my friends, the moments that
173 taught us, forgive me,
    to come
174 together, like birthdays & lectures.
    imagine! someone devoting a life to
175 teach what we will all forget. we kept
    our word, didn't attempt to
176 tamper with anything more, buried
    this here capsule of us for you.

A Book Reminds Me I've Known Joy

I know love because I have turned the page
of this borrowed book to find a stain of maybe ketchup

or another bright food & I am holding something someone
would not even let go of to eat

I have laughed so hard at a joke I had to clutch a table
for balance   I have smiled so hard I removed

my glasses to make room for my cheeks   I have been so
overwhelmed with gratitude I pulled the car

over & cried at the wheel   I do not have to guess
what it feels like to be this book, admired,

invested in dearly   I have been so tenderly held

Tomorrow, will you remind me? I have been so
tenderly held

Publications

"Black Girl Catholic" appears in *Solstice Literary Magazine*

"Possession" appears in *ColorBloq Magazine*

"Jesus Saves" & "Three Churches Burn in Louisiana" appear in *Washington Square Review*

"Three Churches Burn in Louisiana" appears in *Best New Poets*

"Directions for Breaking Apart" appears in Florida State University's *Pandemic Book Project*

"The Poem in Which We All Go Back to Where We Came From" appears in *The Offing Mag*

"What You Must Do" appears in *TRACK//FOUR Journal*

"From Her Laugh" & "From Her God" appear in *the poet's billow*

A version of "What To Do When There's Nothing You Can Do" appears in *the poet's billow*

"How I Know Things Are Bad Again" appears in *Cosmonaut's Avenue*

"MAYBE:GOD" & "Sanctity: An Expose" appear in *Anomaly*

"Psalm 161" appears in *Tinderbox*

Acknowledgments

While writing these poems, I realized that very few coffee shops have all five of the elements I prioritize: good coffee, good food, accessible outlets, natural lighting, & outside space. So, shoutout to Urban Grind Coffeehouse in Atlanta for checking off every box & being such a comfortable and welcoming writing environment. Major thank you to the friends and family members who uplifted me over the years it took to bring this project to life; to Channa Childs for being the first reader of the very first draft & providing invaluable feedback; to people who saw early drafts of poems & told me when my lines weren't hittin; to Amy Bishop for being the best possible agent; & to the thoughtful editors at Andrews McMeel. Very special thanks to the Barbara Deming Memorial Fund, The Granum Foundation, & The Georgia Writer's Association for believing in this book.

About the Author

Jae Nichelle began competing in poetry slams at 15 years old, becoming one of the inaugural winners of Youth Speaks' national Raise Up competition at 17. Her poetry has appeared in *The Offing Magazine*, *Muzzle Magazine*, *The Washington Square Review*, and elsewhere. Additionally, her viral spoken word piece about anxiety, "Friends With Benefits," has amassed millions of views and counting.

Jae has a passion for language, linguistics, and mental health, and she has published articles in *AFROPUNK*, *An Injustice*, and Black Youth Project on these subjects. Find more of her work at jaenichelle.com and find her on socials @croptopassassin.

Andrews McMeel Publishing
a division of Andrews McMeel Universal
1130 Walnut Street, Kansas City, Missouri 64106

www.andrewsmcmeel.com

23 24 25 26 27 VEP 10 9 8 7 6 5 4 3 2 1

ISBN: 978-1-5248-7840-5

Library of Congress Control Number: 2022946313

Editor: Danys Mares
Art Director/Designer: Diane Marsh
Production Editor: Lauren Manoy
Production Manager: Shona Burns

ATTENTION: SCHOOLS AND BUSINESSES
Andrews McMeel books are available at quantity discounts with bulk purchase for educational, business, or sales promotional use. For information, please e-mail the Andrews McMeel Publishing Special Sales Department: sales@amuniversal.com.